Snakes of North America

Billy Grinslott & Kinsey Marie Books

ISBN - 9781965098523

I0115154

Garter snakes are usually recognized by their yellow stripes. Garter snakes give birth to live young, unlike most snakes that lay eggs. Garter snakes hibernate in large groups from late October to early May. Garter snakes live in a variety of habitats, including woodlands, meadows, and grassy knolls, and they like to be near water. Garter snakes can range in size from 18 to 51 inches in length. Garter snakes are poisonous, but the effects are medically insignificant and unlikely to harm humans. Garter snakes have an excellent sense of smell, which they use to detect predators and prey.

Western hognose snakes live in open prairies, meadows, and flood plains in central North America. Western hognose snakes have an upturned snout, which they use to dig in loose soil kike a hog. When threatened, western hognose snakes will flatten out their necks, inflate their bodies, and hiss. They may also strike at an intruder with their mouth closed. Western hognose snakes eat frogs, toads, salamanders, rodents, lizards, other small snakes, and eggs. Bites from western hognose snakes can cause symptoms such as pain, nausea, bleeding, and blistering.

The name kingsnake comes from the fact that they hunt and eat other snakes, which is rare for most snakes. Kingsnakes are powerful constrictors meaning that they wrap themselves around their prey and kill their prey by suffocation. Kingsnakes have bright colors and bands that flash when they move quickly, which can startle and confuse other animals. Kingsnakes eat a variety of animals, including rodents, birds, lizards, frogs, salamanders, and other snakes. Kingsnakes live in the western parts of America. Kingsnakes are among the smartest of the snake species. Their average size is between 3 to 5 feet long.

Coral snakes live in wooded, sandy, and marshy areas. They eat lizards, frogs, and smaller snakes, including other coral snakes. They are venomous and are part of the elapine species. They are relatives of the cobra, mamba, and sea snake. They have two caution colors, red and yellow, which can be used as a warning to stay away. They generally only bite humans when handled or stepped on. When threatened, they may curl the tip of their tail and release gas from their cloaca to startle predators. Coral snakes are typically 2 to 3 feet long but can grow to 4 feet long.

Pine snakes spend most of their time underground in burrows that they dig. They have small heads and a pointed nose and a thick neck that helps them to burrow into the ground. They hunt underground as well by raiding rodent burrows. Their color ranges from yellowish tan to white to gray or rusty brown. The Pine Snake is believed to be the rarest snake in North America. Adults can reach up to six feet in length. Pine snakes are non-venomous constrictors, but they are known to be aggressive and can deliver a powerful strike. They hiss loudly and vibrate their tails before striking.

The eastern indigo snake is the longest native snake in North America. It can grow up to 9 feet long and weigh up to 3 pounds. The eastern indigo snake is non-venomous and eats a variety of animals, including other snakes, small mammals, birds, toads, frogs, turtles, lizards, and small alligators. The eastern indigo snake is immune to the venom of other snakes and rattlesnakes. When threatened, the eastern indigo snake flattens out its neck, hisses, and vibrates its tail. The eastern indigo snake has iridescent blue-black scales and a coral-colored chin, throat, and cheeks. The eastern indigo snake likes to live in pine forest areas.

Gopher snakes are known for keeping rodent populations under control in agricultural areas. Their name is because they like to feed on rodents, like gophers. Gopher Snakes are large and heavy-bodied reptiles, reaching lengths of eight feet long. Gopher snakes live in a wide variety of habitats across North America. Gopher snakes from different habitats have different colors to help camouflage themselves with the local plants. When threatened, gopher snakes will flatten out their heads, vibrate their tails, and hiss loudly to imitate rattlesnakes. This is because they look like rattlesnakes, but they are not venomous.

Ribbon snakes are very sensitive to vibrations in the ground and have very sharp vision. They have yellow stripes against a black or dark brown body color. Ribbon snakes are good swimmers and like to live around water. They feed on tadpoles, small frogs, and small fishes. Ribbon snakes are related to Garter Snakes but are more tolerant to colder temperatures. Ribbon snakes can range in size from 16 to 41 inches long. They are not venomous. They are fast and use their speed to chase and capture prey.

Smooth green snakes also known as the grass snakes are green on top, white or pale yellow on the belly, and have a white underside on their head. Smooth green snakes live in open areas with grass and shrubs, like fields, lawns, and gardens. They can also be found in grasslands along the edges of woods. Smooth green snakes eat spiders, caterpillars, crickets, and other insects. The smooth green snake is a small to medium-sized snake that typically grows to be 14–24 inches long. Smooth green snakes are not venomous.

The Sidewinder is a rattlesnake. It got its name because it crawls in a sideways pattern. Sidewinders can move up to 18 miles per hour, making them one of the fastest snakes in the world. Sidewinders have very large fangs for a rattlesnake. The raised scales above their eyes resemble horns, it's believed that these horns may help protect the snake's eyes from the sun. Sidewinders eat rodents, lizards, and birds. Sidewinders hibernate during the winter. Sidewinder rattlesnakes can be found in sandy desert areas. Sidewinder rattlesnakes grow to 32 inches long. Sidewinders have venom, but it's weaker than other rattlesnakes. A bite can still be dangerous and require immediate medical attention.

Eastern racers color varies from cream to bright yellow. Eastern racers use their speed and agility to catch their prey. They are known to periscope, by raising their heads above the ground to get a better view of their surroundings. Eastern racers eat a variety of animals, including rodents, frogs, toads, lizards, snakes, eggs, and birds. They live in the eastern United States. They are commonly found in open habitats like grasslands, prairies, and agricultural areas. When threatened, they will coil and strike while shaking their tail nervously. They are not venomous snakes. They can grow to 6 feet long.

The copperhead is about 3 feet long. It has a pinkish or reddish body, with darker bands or blotches. Copperheads live in a variety of habitats, including forests, mixed woodlands, rock outcroppings, and low-lying, swampy regions. Copperheads have pit organs on either side of their head that help them locate objects that are warmer than their surroundings. Copperheads are venomous snakes. Their bites are painful and can cause tissue damage, but they are not fatal.

Cottonmouths get their name from the white interior of their mouths, which they expose when threatened. They are also known as water moccasins. Cottonmouths are usually brown, olive, or black with dark crossbands and light centers. Cottonmouths can grow to 48 inches long. Cottonmouths are semiaquatic, so they're comfortable both swimming in water and being on land. They are found in many areas throughout the USA. When threatened, they will vibrate their tail, throw their head back, and hiss. They may also secrete a strong odor from their anal glands. Cottonmouths are venomous and have fangs that are like tiny needles. However, they can also deliver a dry bite with no venom.

Tiger rattlesnakes got their name from their stripes. Tiger rattlesnakes have the smallest heads of any rattlesnake. Tiger rattlesnakes have one of the most toxic venoms of any rattlesnake. Their venom contains neurotoxins and mycotoxins that cause your muscles to deteriorate. Tiger rattlesnakes live in a variety of habitats, including grasslands, thorn scrub, oak forests, and hill areas. Tiger rattlesnakes are usually mild-tempered and unlikely to strike, but they will attack if agitated. Tiger rattlesnakes can grow to be 36 inches long.

Diamondback rattlesnakes got their name because they have diamond shaped patches. The Diamondback can exceed seven feet in length and is king of the desert rattlers. They are classified as pit vipers because of facial pits found below and between the eye and nostril on both sides of the head. Diamondbacks are ambush predators that use their sense of smell and infrared detection to find prey. They strike their prey with their curved fangs, injecting venom that kills red blood cells and damages tissue. Diamondbacks use their rattles to warn off predators and humans. The rattle is made of keratin, the same material as fingernails, and is a series of interlocking segments that vibrate when shaken. The snake adds a new part to its rattle each time it sheds its skin. Diamondback venom is a potent hemotoxin that can be fatal to humans.

Timber rattlesnakes got their name because they like to live in forested areas. Timber rattlesnakes are found from Canada to Texas. They are the only rattlesnake species in most of the Northern United States. They can grow to be over five feet long. Timber rattlesnakes are venomous. Their bites can cause severe facial and nerve paralysis, shock, and coagulopathy, which means your blood will not clot to plug off the wounded area. Timber rattlesnakes can recognize their siblings, even if they were separated at birth.

There are several types of Garter Snakes, and they all have different colors and markings depending on what part of North America you live in. They also go by different names, but they are all part of the Garter Snake family. Garter snakes are viviparous, meaning they give birth to live young instead of laying eggs. Garter snakes hibernate in communities, sometimes with hundreds of snakes, from October to April.

The Mojave Rattlesnake is also known as the Mojave Green Rattlesnake. Mojave rattlesnakes can be greenish, brownish, or yellowish, with darker patches on their backs. Mojave rattlesnakes live in arid habitats like desert flatlands, creosote bush, cacti, mesquite, and Joshua tree woodlands. Mojave rattlesnakes are mainly nocturnal and during the heat of the day hide in burrows or under rocks. The Mojave rattlesnake has two pits between its eyes and nostrils that help it find prey in the dark. During cooler days they may come out to bask in the sun. They are most active from April to September and hibernate alone or in small groups during the winter. The Mojave rattlesnake's venom is poisonous.

Massasauga Rattlesnakes. The name massasauga comes from the Ojibwe word for great river mouth. Massasaugas live in the northern Midwest United States and Canada. Massasaugas do not always rattle to make their presence known. They are good swimmers and can hunt their prey in the water. They detect prey with smell and with the help of heat-sensitive pits located on their faces. They can also feel vibrations and have good eyesight.

Speckled rattlesnakes come in many colors, including pink, orange, brown, gray, and yellow. Their color helps them blend in with their environment. Speckled rattlesnakes live in rocky habitats in the Mojave and Sonoran Deserts. Speckled rattlesnakes are usually 24 to 30 inches long but can grow to be 36 inches long. The Speckled rattlesnake is a venomous pit viper species.

Pygmy rattlesnakes are small, venomous snakes that are usually 15 to 24 inches long. They are common in the southeastern USA, and are often found in rocky, partially wooded hillsides. They use a sit-and-wait method to hunt lizards, frogs, rodents, and insects. Their venom is hemorrhagic, which means it causes tissue damage. Their rattle sounds like a buzzing insect. They are not aggressive and usually avoid contact with people.

The Ridge Nosed Rattlesnakes name comes from the upturned scales that run along the side of their nose. Ridge Nosed rattlesnakes are small, rarely growing longer than 24 inches. They mainly live in the mountain areas of Arizona and New Mexico. Their venom is not very toxic and poses a low threat to humans if bitten. The snake is active mostly in the daytime, often basking on rocks in the sunlight. The ridge-nosed rattlesnake is the state reptile of Arizona.

Water snakes are non-venomous and are part of the colubrid family, which is the most common and largest family of snakes. Water snakes can be found in many different habitats, including bogs, swamps, slow-moving rivers, and ponds. Water snakes are often confused with water moccasins and cottonmouths. Water snakes are strong swimmers and can stay underwater for long periods of time. Water snakes eat fish, frogs, crayfish, salamanders, small turtles, other snakes, small mammals, and birds. Water snakes can bite repeatedly, more than one time, and their bite is painful.

Black-tailed rattlesnakes live in rocky areas, canyons, and cliffs in the mountains of Arizona, Mexico, and Texas. Black-tailed rattlesnakes move by slithering, side-winding, or rectilinear movement. They can also climb trees and swim quickly. Black-tailed rattlesnakes are considered to be one of the most docile rattlesnakes because of their calm demeanor.

Crotalus Lepidus is a group of venomous pit viper rattlesnake species found in the southwestern USA, and northern Mexico. They include banded rock rattlesnakes, blue rattlesnakes, green or green rock rattlesnakes, and rock rattlesnakes.

Red diamond rattlesnakes are named for their bright red color and distinctive, white-bordered diamond pattern on their backs. They live in rocky shorelines, canyons, desert slopes, and hillsides in the southwestern United States. They can grow to be over 64 inches long. They are primarily nocturnal but can be seen basking in the sun during cooler parts of the year. They use their rattles to warn off potential threats. Their venom is harmful to humans and other prey.

Gray-banded kingsnakes are fascinating snakes known for their unique color variations, and their ability to adapt to harsh desert environments. They are also known for their relatively wide head compared to other kingsnakes. Their color can vary, with shades of gray with orange or red bands. During hot summers, they enter a state of hibernation to conserve energy and survive the extreme heat. They are not poisonous and are considered docile. They can reach lengths of up to 4 feet.

Short-tailed snakes are native to Florida's central peninsula, where they live in dry sandhills and scrub habitats. Short-tailed snakes are small and slender. It can reach 20 inches long with a cylindrical body that transitions into its head. Short-tailed snakes are non-venomous and will eat other small snakes. Short-tailed snakes are mostly nocturnal and live underground.

Red-bellied snakes are brown or gray with a red or pink underside. Red-bellied snakes are small, nonvenomous snakes that are about the size of a large nightcrawler. They grow to be ten inches long. Red-bellied snakes eat slugs, earthworms, snails, grubs, and insects. Red-bellied snakes live in woodlands, forest edges, fields, meadows, and near water. They also live in logs, rocks, scrap piles, and building foundations.

Queen snakes are slender snakes that are brownish to olive-green in color. They have a cream-colored stripe on their lower body and head. Queen snakes are not large, they seldom grow to more than 24 inches in length. Queen snakes will thrash, spin, and secrete a foul-smelling musk if threatened. Queen snakes are not poisonous and are not dangerous to humans or pets. Queen snakes like to live near water. Queen snakes are docile and will drop into water if disturbed. Queen snakes like to eat crayfish and other small critters.

Long nosed snakes have a longer, pointed nose than other Kingsnakes. If disturbed or threatened, long nosed won't bite but they will release a foul-smelling musk and blood from the cloaca as a defense mechanism. Long-nosed snakes are burrowing snakes that live in deserts, grasslands, shrublands, and prairies. Long-nosed snakes are related to and sometimes similar in appearance to the Kingsnake. Long-nosed snakes can grow to be 32 inches long.

Coachwhip Snakes are a non-venomous snake that's native to the USA, and Mexico. The name comes from the snake's long, thin tail, which has large scales that make it look like a braided whip. Coachwhip snakes are long and slender and can grow to be over 8 feet long. They are most found in open habitats with sandy soil, such as prairies, old fields, and coastal dunes. Coachwhips are extremely fast, able to move at speeds of up to 10 miles per hour. Coachwhips are curious but sensitive to threats and will often scurry off at the first sign of danger. Coachwhips are excellent climbers, often taking shelter in small trees or brush.

Rat snakes are named after their primary food source, rats and mice. Rat snakes are helpful in controlling the rodent population. Rat snakes can grow to be 8 feet long, making them one of the longest snakes in North America. There are many types of rat snakes, including the black, the eastern, and the rhinoceros rat snake. They are non-venomous. When threatened, rat snakes will rattle their tails to trick other animals into thinking they are venomous. They are docile and slow, and may discharge a foul liquid, or strike if they are frightened.

The corn snake gets its name from its association with corn fields and corn cribs where it hunts for rats and other rodents. Corn snakes are beneficial to humans because they help control rodent populations. Corn snakes can grow to be six feet long, with females generally being larger than males. Corn snakes are nocturnal. They are active, curious, and can be escape artists. Corn snakes are not venomous, but they can bite if they feel threatened or smell food. Corn snakes are constrictors, which squeeze and suffocate their prey.

Crowned snakes have a dark spot on their head, that's how they got their name. Crowned snakes rarely grow longer than 28 inches long. Crowned snakes have small fangs that inject venom into their prey. Their venom is potent and paralyzing. Crowned snakes are not considered a threat to humans because of their small size and reclusive nature. They are normally found in the southeastern parts of the USA. They Primarily eat beetles, snails, centipedes, and spiders.

Ring-necked snakes got their name because they have a ring around their neck. Ring-necked snakes are also known as Corkscrew snakes because they coil their tails over their bodies to expose their bright underside when threatened. Ring-necked snakes have soft, skin-like scales that don't retain moisture well, so they live in damp environments. Ring-necked snakes are venomous, but their venom is harmless to humans.

Twin Spotted Rattlesnakes got their name because they have two rolls of spots on their back. The Twin Spotted Rattlesnake is primarily found in the high mountain regions of southeastern Arizona and parts of Mexico. Due to their secluded mountain habitat, encounters with Twin Spotted Rattlesnakes are uncommon. It primarily feeds on lizards and is considered a relatively shy snake. Considered a small rattlesnake, adults typically reach only up to 2 feet in length. Their venom is highly toxic, but they are not known for biting humans.

Fun Facts About Snakes

Snakes have a strong sense of smell and use their forked tongue to pick up scents. Snakes have a strong sense of taste.

Snakes don't have eyelids. Instead, they have a thin membrane called a "brille" to protect their eyes.

Snakes have internal ears but no external ears.

Snakes have flexible jaws that can stretch in multiple directions. This allows them to swallow prey that is much larger than their head.

Snakes shed their skin multiple times a year.

About 70% of snakes lay eggs, the others give birth to live young.

Most snakes have poor eyesight and can only see shapes.

Some snakes are poisonous and use venom to kill their prey.

Some sea snakes can breathe partially through their skin, allowing them to dive underwater for long periods.

Snakes come in many different sizes.

Snakes live on every continent except Antarctica.

Author Page

Billy Grinslott & Kinsey Marie Books

Copyright, All Rights Reserved

ISBN – 9781965098523

Thanks

www.ingramcontent.com/pod-product-compliance
Lightning Source LLC
Chambersburg PA
CBHW060833270326
41933CB00002B/71